Memorize Math Facts in Minutes with the

Number Town
Numbers

Written by Cambria and Jackie Brann

Illustrated by Cambria Brann

www.numbertownnumbers.com

About the Book

Number Town Numbers was created to help students who struggle when memorizing math facts. This book was designed to help them learn their multiplication facts within weeks and creates an easy recall system to retrieve the information from their long-term memory.

How does it work?

*Each Number Town number has a unique personality with silly stories and adventures throughout the book.

*The Number Town Numbers stories have a particular cadence pattern that allows the brain to better encode and recall the math facts.

*Number Town Numbers repeats the newly learned math facts multiple times throughout the story. This repetition helps anchor the information in the long-term memory.

*Number Town Numbers contains a built in mnemonic device that optimizes the math facts storage and retrieval within the student's long-term memory.

The Number Town Numbers book is a must-have book for every 1st - 3rd grade classroom. It is also a fun at-home math enhancement tool that helps students master math facts quickly and efficiently.

Introducing...

The Number Town Numbers

Once upon a time, in a tiny little nook,
There was a secret town, by a tiny little brook.
You can't just go and find it,
You must know where to look.
You'll find the special numbers, not kept in any book.
Memorizing numbers can be a gruesome bore,
The figures swirl around your head,
Until you hit the floor.
But come on down to Number Town,
We'll open up our door,
Meet our friends and hear their tales,
You'll roll your eyes no more.
For the numbers in this special town,
Math facts are so much fun.
The first new friend you'll meet today,
Is cheerful Number One!

Number One

The first new friend you'll meet today
Is cheerful Number ONE.
She's always on the go; she's always on the run.
She's happy and she's helpful,
Our dear friend Number ONE.
She waves a big foam finger,
Smiling brightly, like the sun.

Number Two

As we go through the town, to meet them all,
We're sure to find TWO hanging out at the mall.
TWO loves her shoes, and buys them in pairs,
She lines them all up, on the front of her stairs.
She skip counts her way, to her room at the top,
With so many shoes, she could open a shop.

Number Three

Next door to Two, lives old Granny THREE,
Who passes her days sitting up in a tree.
She wakes in the morning, she's soon sipping tea,
Enjoying fresh air with her good friend the bee.
Granny THREE is not lonely, she's a happy old gal.
She always sips tea with a good friend or pal.

Number Four

Here comes FOUR bouncing his ball,
Through Granny's door and right down the hall.
Her grandson is playful and always wants more,
With his skills on the field FOUR is ready to score!
He knows all the rules and always plays fair,
To see him sit still, is super rare.

Number Five

As we continue our stroll down this magical street,
Buzzing number FIVE is next that we meet.
Surrounded by bees, that's how you'll find FIVE,
His big-domed house looks like a huge yellow hive.
He's constantly cleaning and running about,
The busiest number, without any doubt.

Number Six

Listen now, as you can hear,
It's the house of SIX that we are near.
SIX on sticks plays drums in a band,
With spiky hair and a stick in each hand.
SIX on sticks will make you rock,
But use the bell; he won't hear you knock.

Number Seven

Six's sister is Sweet Singin' SEVEN,
She's usually found with her big dog Kevin.
Her voice, though its pretty, can be hard to hear,
When her brother Six is drumming so near.
So listen now for the sweet voice of SEVEN,
It sounds like it comes straight down from heaven.

Number Eight

If you get hungry in town there's no need to worry,
Skateboarding EIGHT brings food in a hurry.
With pizza, french fries, and cookies galore,
EIGHT will deliver them straight to your door.
He knows the town well, forwards and back,
From the biggest hotel to the most humble shack.

Number Nine

With her dojo located at the end of the street,
It's Ninja NINE you are lucky to meet.
Ninja NINE moves so quickly with her martial arts,
The most brilliant of fighters she simply outsmarts.
With her mask tied so tightly, hiding her eyes,
She can take down opponents no matter their size.

Multiplying With...

The Number Town Numbers

So now you've met the numbers,
You know their quirky ways,
You know their favorite hobbies,
And how they spend their days.
It's time to see them mingle now,
And hang out with their friends,
This is how they multiply,
Not how their story ends.
We can walk the streets of Number Town,
Crisscrossing back and forth,
We'll enter at the south of town,
And make our way up north.

Number One

Let's learn the facts now, starting with ONE,
She loves trying new things and having big fun.
She goes right along with what others like,
Such as drawing and fishing or riding a bike.
ONE will be there, to play with her friends,
Her list of good times just never ends.

When multiplying a number, by our good friend ONE,
There is nothing that changes, isn't that fun?

ONE times a number won't change a thing,
You're learning so quickly it's starting to ZING!
ONE times a number, no change up or down,
It makes ONE so special, in our number town!

Number Two

Now that you know our good friend One,
Let's meet a number that's twice as much fun!
She lives in a castle of beautiful blues,
And she dearly loves her collection of shoes!
Skip counting is fun, it's numbers in pairs,
It's easy to do when skipping up stairs.

TWO's a collector, collecting in pairs,
Always skip counting the shoes that she wears.
With so many colors, she loves every pair,
She loves to skip count as she goes anywhere.
Her rule is quite simple counting by TWOs,
In every pair, she has double the shoes.

Number Three

Now that you've met our fun family tree,
Let's start to multiply with Dear Granny THREE.
She loves big adventure; her best friend is a bee,
She always has stories that fill us with glee.
The Number Town locals all seem to enjoy,
Her world famous tea, mixed with honey and soy.

$$3 \times 2 = 6$$

Sweet number TWO, the girl from the mall,
Sips tea with granny while wearing her shawl.
Granny THREE has the choices, too many to choose,
Like strawberry herbal that wont match her shoes.

*Chai heel tea is the one that she **picks**.*
*THREE **times** TWO **is equal to** SIX.*
(picks = 6)

$$3 \times 3 = 9$$

So Two went home to rest and lay down,
Guess who showed up in our Number Town?
Granny THREE's twin sister, Miss Nana THREE,
Brought jars of honey from her bumblebee.

*She takes a slow sip, the tea is **divine**.*
*THREE **times** THREE **is always** NINE.*
(divine = 9)

3 x 4 = 12

Granny THREE is excited; it's a great day!
Her grandson FOUR is now on his way.
After scoring a goal to win the big game,
Coach gave him a trophy, engraved with his name.

*The trophy is placed on top of the **shelves.***
*THREE **times** FOUR **can only be** TWELVE.*
(shelves = 12)

3 x 5 = 15

Granny THREE takes her tea to East Honey Drive,
And visits her good friend, 'ol number FIVE.
His bright yellow house is perfect you see,
Holding special events for fine royalty.

*Granny THREE brings tea fit for a **queen**.*
THREE *times* FIVE *is* FIFTEEN.
(queen = 15)

3 x 6 = 18

Granny THREE loves baking with SIX on sticks,
His humor and charm are such a good mix.
SIX bangs his drums real loud while she's mixing,
The pounding in her head will soon need some fixing.

*Poor Granny's head really starts **aching**.*
*THREE **times** SIX **is equal to** EIGHTEEN.*
(aching = 18)

3 x 7 = 21

THREE helps SEVEN perform every spring,
The number town musical is where she will sing.
When SEVEN gets nervous she needs a treat,
Granny runs to the store, right down the street.

*Granny comes back with candy, and **minty gum.***
*THREE **times** SEVEN **is** TWENTY-ONE.*
(minty gum = 21)

3 x 8 = 24

EIGHT handed out pizza, all different brands,
The food was quite greasy it lubed up his hands.
He heads over to visit with Dear Granny THREE,
With slippery hands, he dropped the tea.

Poor Granny THREE with a now **denty floor.**
THREE **times** *EIGHT* **is** *TWENTY-FOUR.*
(denty floor = 24)

3 x 9 = 27

Ninja NINE and Dear Granny THREE,
They drink something different than her usual tea.
NINE cut the lemons with a super sharp blade,
THREE squeezed them all to make lemonade.

She sharpened her sword and cut **plenty of lemons.**
THREE **times** *NINE is TWENTY-SEVEN.*
(plenty of lemons = 27)

Number Four

Multiplication!! It's not such a bore,
So now let's move on, multiplying by FOUR.
He's the finest of athletes in 200 miles,
Every time that he scores there's plenty of smiles
So now lets watch FOUR on our local streets,
Having fun and competing with each number he meets.

4 x 2 = 8

FOUR hits the ice, he's graceful you'd say,
Performing with skills in his FOUR kind of way.
But TWO kept on sliding all over the place,
Slipping and falling without any grace.

She needs more practice if she's gonna **skate.**
FOUR **times** TWO **is always** EIGHT.
(skate = 8)

4 x 3 = 12

Granny THREE is excited, it's a great day!
Her grandson FOUR is now on his way.
After scoring a goal to win the big game,
Coach gave him a trophy, engraved with his name.

*The trophy is placed on top of the **shelves.***
*FOUR **times** THREE **can only be** TWELVE.*
(shelves = 12)

4 x 4 = 16

FOUR is prepared on the ice to play,
All by himself and his mind today.
FOUR ate a quick snack, a burger and fries,
Looking back on his choice, it wasn't that wise.

FOUR spins too fast and becomes a **sick teen.**
FOUR times FOUR equals SIXTEEN.
(sick teen = 16)

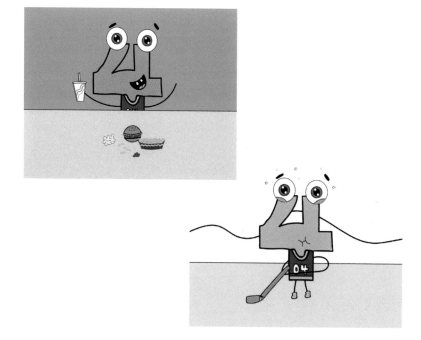

4 x 5 = 20

FOUR goes out with his friend for a dive,
Yep, you guessed it, he's hanging with FIVE.
He's taking a break from all of his bees,
And the two look for oysters under the seas.

Down in the reef, they find **plenty.**
FOUR *times* FIVE **equals** TWENTY.
(plenty = 20)

4 x 6 = 24

A big storm is brewing with a crack and a boom,
So FOUR and his pal played ball in his room.
SIX tried to show off and threw it too fast,
Hitting the door as the ball went past.

It bounced off the wall and hit the now **dented door.**
FOUR times SIX is TWENTY-FOUR.
(dented door = 24)

4 x 7 = 28

FOUR likes a new challenge every once in a while,
So he approached SEVEN while wearing a smile.
The singing was starting, downtown at the school,
If they missed the contest, it wouldn't be cool.

He knew he must hurry or **he'd be late.**
FOUR **times** *SEVEN* **is** *TWENTY-EIGHT.*
(he'd be late = 28)

4 x 8 = 32

When it rains in town, there's not much to do,
FOUR and EIGHT only skate when skies are blue.
The last raindrop falls and FOUR hits the ground,
Ignoring the fact that there's mud all around!

*The mud where he stepped gave him one **dirty shoe**.*
*FOUR **times** EIGHT **is** THIRTY-TWO.*
(dirty shoe = 32)

4 x 9 = 36

That same rainy night, FOUR went to see NINE,
He thought that ninja looked pretty fine.
Sneaking up on her quietly, flowers in hand,
Flat on his back, he quickly did land.

NINE pinned FOUR down for his **flirty tricks.**
FOUR *times* **NINE** *is* THIRTY-SIX.
(flirty tricks = 36)

Number Five

Now let's head over to the big yellow hive,
Inside we will look, to find number FIVE.
He's really quite famous in our Number Town,
His unique form of magic is known all around.
Much like two, FIVE has a rule,
We think he's special, we think he's cool.
You see five's have no choice, they disappear,
An even number will do it, that much is clear.

5 x 2 = 10

TWO loves FIVE because his shoes are for running,
He's always so busy, his chores are just stunning.
He sprints all around as if he is late,
She slows him down to meditate.

*She calms her breath and reaches **Zen**.*
*FIVE **times** TWO **is equal to** TEN.*
(Zen = 10)

5 x 3 = 15

Granny THREE takes her tea to East Honey Drive,
And visits her good friend, 'ol number FIVE.
His bright yellow house is perfect you see,
Holding special events for fine royalty.

Granny THREE brings tea fit for a **queen.**
FIVE **times** *THREE* **is** *FIFTEEN.*
(queen = 15)

5 x 4 = 20

FOUR goes out with his friend for a dive,
Yep, you guessed it, he's hanging with FIVE.
He's taking a break from all of his bees,
And the two look for oysters under the seas.

*Down in the reef, they find **plenty.***
*FIVE **times** FOUR **equals** TWENTY.*
(plenty = 20)

5 x 5 = 25

FIVE loves his bees, and the bees all love FIVE,
When his friends are all buzzing he feels alive.
He feeds them, they're healthy, they never get sick,
He's careful and thorough; it's no magic trick.

He treats them well and **plenty thrive.**
FIVE **times** *FIVE is* TWENTY-FIVE.
(plenty thrive = 25)

5 x 6 = 30

SIX came to see FIVE and all of the bees,
The bees were all buzzing and started to sneeze.
Both SIX and FIVE were covered in honey,
They fell to the floor 'cause it was so funny.

*Rolling and laughing they got really **dirty.***
*FIVE **times** SIX **is equal to** THIRTY.*
*(**dirty** = 30)*

5 x 7 = 35

She sings as she walks, her voice straight from heaven,
FIVE has a crush on Sweet Singin' SEVEN.
FIVE is in love, this much is true,
Poor little SEVEN, has not a clue.

*She sings as she passes his **sturdy hive.***
*FIVE **times** SEVEN **is** THIRTY-FIVE.*
(sturdy hive = 35)

5 x 8 = 40

FIVE scrubbing his roof, way up high,
He sees EIGHT below, delivering chicken potpie.
From up on the roof, EIGHT looks so tiny,
FIVE wants to be noticed, his roof is so shiny.

*He giggles and yells out, "Hey there, **shorty!**"*
*FIVE **times** EIGHT **is equal to** FORTY.*
(shorty = 40)

$$5 \times 9 = 45$$

Enjoying his lunch and watching the bees,
It's a bright yellow sign that number FIVE sees.
Come join NINE for a FREE ninja class,
It comes once a year so you don't want to pass.

*He follows the sign to East **Sporty Drive**.*
*FIVE **times** NINE **is** FORTY-FIVE.*
(Sporty Drive = 45)

Number Six

SIX taps out beats wherever he can,
He bangs on the stove, on rocks or a pan.
He's really got rhythm as he taps out his beat,
He stomps out the bass line using his feet.
It's all about music with this rockin' boy,
Keeping the beat is ultimate joy.

6 x 2 = 12

TWO went with SIX, shopping for shoes,
But the pair that she picked was sparkly blues.
SIX did not like them, not one little bit,
TWO couldn't argue, they just weren't a fit.

*Sadly she placed them back on the **shelves.***
***SIX** times **TWO** is equal to* TWELVE.
(shelves = 12)

6 x 3 = 18

Granny THREE loves baking with SIX on sticks,
His humor and charm are such a good mix.
SIX bangs his drums real loud while she's mixing,
The pounding in her head will soon need some fixing.

*Poor Granny's head really starts **aching.***
*SIX **times** THREE **is equal to** EIGHTEEN.*
(aching = 18)

6 x 4 = 24

A big storm is brewing with a crack and a boom,
So FOUR and his pal played ball in his room.
SIX tried to show off and threw it too fast,
Hitting the door as the ball went past.

*It bounced off the wall and hit the now **dented** door.*
*SIX **times** FOUR is TWENTY-FOUR.*
(dented door = 24)

6 x 5 = 30

SIX came to see FIVE and all of the bees,
The bees were all buzzing and started to sneeze.
Both SIX and FIVE were covered in honey,
They fell to the floor 'cause it was so funny.

*Rolling and laughing they got really **dirty**.*
*SIX **times** FIVE **is equal to** THIRTY.*
(dirty = 30)

6 x 6 = 36

Drumming his way through the quaint little town,
SIX works his sticks and he starts to frown.
Strange, he was thinking, as he suddenly saddened,
His sticks got so dirty and they slowly blackened.

SIX just noticed his **dirty sticks.**
SIX **times** *SIX* **is** *THIRTY-SIX.*
(dirty sticks = 36)

6 x 7 = 42

SEVEN can sing and her cooking's divine,
SIX was so hungry he started to whine.
SEVEN feeds SIX to play drums for her show,
Without a good meal his beat doesn't flow.

*SEVEN made SIX a thick **hearty stew.***
*SIX **times** SEVEN **is** FORTY-TWO.*
(hearty stew = 42)

6 x 8 = 48

SIX seems a bit clumsy and hates to be late,
He must find a teacher to teach him to skate.
He begs and he pleads, will EIGHT teach him how?
He really just wants to jump over a cow!

*SIX has no watch, and is **always late!***
***SIX** times EIGHT **must be** FORTY-EIGHT.*
(always late = 48)

6 x 9 = 54

SIX is really nervous and super scared of NINE,
He's really just afraid that she'll break his fragile spine.
He's timid and he's fearful, as he steps upon the mat,
Nothing else was heard... except a vicious SPLAT!

*In one smooth move SIX **hits the floor.***
*SIX **times** NINE **is** FIFTY-FOUR.*
(hits the floor = 54)

Number Seven

Sweet Singin' SEVEN, the Number Town performer,
Putting on plays when the weather gets warmer.
Her talents are strong and quite entertaining,
The crowd gets excited and might need restraining.
It's time for a musical, and all is just right,
Now we join the numbers and watch her show tonight.

7 x 2 = 14

SEVEN's dress has been pressed, now it's so clean,
The opening act looks pretty keen.
TWO starts to panic, one shoe isn't shining,
The right shoe is done, the left caused the whining.

*She scrubs it and buffs it; the left shoe is **more clean.***
*SEVEN **times** TWO **is always** FOURTEEN.*
(more clean = 14)

7 x 3 = 21

THREE helps SEVEN perform every spring,
The number town musical is where she will sing.
When SEVEN gets nervous she needs a treat,
Granny runs to the store, right down the street.

Granny comes back with candy, and **minty gum.**
SEVEN **times** *THREE is TWENTY-ONE.*
(minty gum = 21)

7 x 4 = 28

FOUR likes a new challenge every once in a while,
So he approached SEVEN while wearing a smile.
The singing was starting, downtown at the school,
If they missed the contest, it wouldn't be cool.

He knew he must hurry or **he'd be late.**
SEVEN **times** *FOUR* **is** *TWENTY-EIGHT.*
(he'd be late = 28)

7 x 5 = 35

She sings as she walks, her voice straight from heaven,
FIVE has a crush on Sweet Singin' SEVEN.
FIVE is in love, this much is true,
Poor little SEVEN, has not a clue.

*She sings as she passes his **sturdy hive.***
*SEVEN **times** FIVE **is** THIRTY-FIVE.*
(sturdy hive = 35)

7 x 6 = 42

SEVEN can sing and her cooking's divine,
SIX was so hungry he started to whine.
SEVEN feeds SIX to play drums for her show,
Without a good meal his beat doesn't flow.

*SEVEN made SIX a thick **hearty stew.***
SEVEN times SIX is FORTY-TWO.
(hearty stew = 42)

7 x 7 = 49

SEVEN isn't ready, to do her thing tonight,
Feeling really nervous, her butterflies take flight.
SEVEN sees the mirror and starts to feel right,
The words come flowing back, so she can sing all night.

*Suddenly she's ready, now it's **party time**.*
*SEVEN **times** SEVEN **is** FORTY-NINE.*
(party time = 49)

7 x 8 = 56

When SEVEN feels nervous she really needs to eat,
Her cravings aren't just weird; they simply can't be beat.
It's fishy sticks that she craves, before she can perform.
Now EIGHT just has to hurry, he can beat the storm.

SEVEN then dines on her **fishy sticks.**
SEVEN **times** *EIGHT* **is** *FIFTY-SIX.*
(fishy sticks = 56)

7 x 9 = 63

SEVEN on stage, with beauty and bling,
She's the star for the night, and ready to sing.
It's Ninja NINE dressed like an old lady,
Searching the crowd for anyone shady.

NINE provides SEVEN with tight **security**.
SEVEN **times** NINE **is** SIXTY-THREE.
(security = 63)

Number Eight

When you get a little hungry, there is no need to worry,
Eight delivers fast, 'cause he's always in a hurry.
He doesn't just sell pizza, fishy sticks or soup,
He delivers everything, pick your best food group.
But it isn't always easy, it usually is not.
Random things can happen, they happen quite a lot.
We'll try our best to keep up, racing through the town,
We can see what happens, as we make our way around.

8 x 2 = 16

EIGHT got a call from his good friend TWO,
Her cousin came over and he had the flu.
TWO wanted him better, her heart is so pure,
She hoped that EIGHT could deliver a cure.

He brought chicken soup just for the **sick teen.**
EIGHT **times** *TWO* **equals** *SIXTEEN.*
(sick teen = 16)

8 x 3 = 24

EIGHT handed out pizza, all different brands,
The food was quite greasy it lubed up his hands.
He heads over to visit with Dear Granny THREE,
With slippery hands, he dropped the tea.

Poor Granny THREE with a now **denty floor.**
EIGHT **times** *THREE* **is** *TWENTY-FOUR.*
(denty floor = 24)

8 x 4 = 32

When it rains in town, there's not much to do,
FOUR and EIGHT only skate when skies are blue.
The last raindrop falls and FOUR hits the ground,
Ignoring the fact that there's mud all around!

The mud where he stepped gave him one **dirty shoe.**
*EIGHT **times** FOUR **is** THIRTY-TWO.*
(dirty shoe = 32)

8 x 5 = 40

FIVE scrubbing his roof, way up high,
He sees EIGHT below, delivering a chicken pot pie.
From up on the roof, EIGHT looks so tiny,
FIVE wants to be noticed, his roof is so shiny.

*He giggles and yells out, "Hey there, **shorty!**"*
*EIGHT **times** FIVE **is equal to** FORTY.*
(shorty = 40)

8 x 6 = 48

SIX seems a bit clumsy and hates to be late,
He must find a teacher to teach him to skate.
He begs and he pleads, will EIGHT teach him how?
He really just wants to jump over a cow!

*SIX has no watch, and is **always late!***
*EIGHT **times** SIX **must be** FORTY-EIGHT.*
(always late = 48)

8 x 7 = 56

When SEVEN feels nervous she really needs to eat,
Her cravings aren't just weird, they simply can't be beat.
It's fishy sticks that she craves, before she can perform.
Now EIGHT just has to hurry, he can beat the storm.

SEVEN then dines on her **fishy sticks.**
EIGHT **times** *SEVEN* **is** *FIFTY-SIX.*
(fishy sticks = 56)

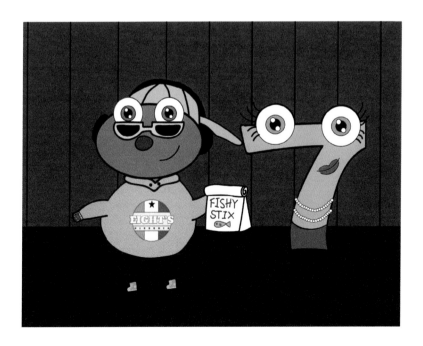

8 x 8 = 64

EIGHT is in a hurry, he's really running late,
EIGHT pies to be delivered, he stacks them on a plate.
The pies start to wiggle, the pies start to drop,
They each hit the ground with a very wet PLOP!

*EIGHT is now left with a very **sticky floor**.*
*EIGHT **times** EIGHT **is** SIXTY-FOUR.*
(sticky floor = 64)

8 x 9 = 72

NINE is super nervous, eating calms her down,
She wants a favorite meal, from the other side of town.
EIGHT knows he can deliver, this is nothing new,
She's so very happy, to receive her favorite brew.

*It's filled to the top, with **heavenly stew.***
*EIGHT **times** NINE **is** SEVENTY-TWO.*
(heavenly stew = 72)

Number Nine

Nine is just amazing, and moves with subtle grace,
She always wears a mask, which covers up her face.
Her clothes are always tidy; she never wears a skirt.
Her mood is never gloomy; she always stays alert.
She frequently is found, in the dojo of this town.
All the locals feel safe; she keeps the crime rate down.

9 x 2 = 18

NINE is a ninja, with no glitter or bows,
Those are slippers she wears, to cover her toes.
Into the dojo comes sweet number TWO,
Her bows both have diamonds on top of each shoe.

*"If you kick me with those my jaw will be **aching**."*
NINE **times** TWO **equals** EIGHTEEN.
(aching = 18)

9 x 3 = 27

Ninja NINE and Dear Granny THREE,
They drink something different than her usual tea.
NINE cut the lemons with a super sharp blade,
THREE squeezed them all to make lemonade.

She sharpened her sword and cut **plenty of lemons.**
NINE **times** *THREE* **is** *TWENTY-SEVEN.*
(plenty of lemons = 27)

9 x 4 = 36

That same rainy night, FOUR went to see NINE,
He thought that ninja looked pretty fine.
Sneaking up on her quietly, flowers in hand,
Flat on his back, he quickly did land.

NINE pinned FOUR down for his **flirty tricks.**
NINE **times** *FOUR* **is** *THIRTY-SIX*.
(flirty tricks = 36)

9 x 5 = 45

Enjoying his lunch and watching the bees,
It's a bright yellow sign that number FIVE sees.
Come join NINE for a FREE ninja class,
It comes once a year so you don't want to pass.

*He follows the sign to East **Sporty Drive**.*
*NINE **times** FIVE **is** FORTY-FIVE.*
(Sporty Drive = 45)

9 x 6 = 54

SIX is really nervous and super scared of NINE,
He's really just afraid that she'll break his fragile spine.
He's timid and he's fearful, as he steps upon the mat,
Nothing else was heard... except a vicious SPLAT!

In one smooth move SIX **hits the floor.**
NINE **times** *SIX is* FIFTY-FOUR.
(hits the floor = 54)

9 x 7 = 63

SEVEN on stage, with beauty and bling,
She's the star for the night, and ready to sing.
It's Ninja NINE dressed like an old lady,
Searching the crowd for anyone shady.

NINE provides SEVEN with the best **security.**
NINE **times** SEVEN **is** *SIXTY-THREE.*
(security = 63)

9 x 8 = 72

NINE is super nervous, eating calms her down,
She wants a favorite meal, from the other side of town.
EIGHT knows he can deliver, this is nothing new,
She's so very happy, to receive her favorite brew.

*It's filled to the top, with **heavenly stew.***
*NINE **times** EIGHT **is** SEVENTY-TWO.*
(heavenly stew = 72)

9 x 9 = 81

NINE stands with pride and reflects in the glass,
A long, long way from that very first class.
NINE found her passion, and worked hard every day,
Ninja NINE was created in a disciplined way.

*She's no longer known as the **"lazy one"**.*
*NINE **times** NINE **is** EIGHTY-ONE.*
(lazy one = 81)

Now that you've finished this book with such ease,
You can state proudly, "Math facts are a breeze!"
We're sad that you're leaving, this is the end,
Make sure to come back, and please bring a friend!

For the *Number Town Numbers* workbook and other activities please go to:

www.numbertownnumbers.com

Made in the USA
Las Vegas, NV
13 December 2020

12789148R00057